Rising Smoke

The Levitical Offerings

An inductive Bible teaching series
for individuals or groups

by Doug Parrington

Rising Smoke - The Levitical Offerings

Published by NENGE BOOKS, Australia, September 2016
ABN 26809396184
Email: nengebooks1@gmail.com
http://nengebooks.com

Unless otherwise indicated, all Scripture quotations are taken from the Holy Bible, New Living Translation, copyright © 1996. Used by permission of Tyndale House Publishers, Inc. Wheaton, Illinois 60189. All rights reserved.

Copyright © Douglas K Parrington 2016
All rights reserved.

Available from bookstores or order direct at wholesale price from the publisher at nengebooks1@gmail.com

Illustrations:
Cover –
    Cross and Fire Wallpaper, free download,
    copyright © http://wallpaper4god.com.
Front page –
    High priest offering a sacrifice of a goat, as on the Day of Atonement, from Henry Davenport Northrop, *Treasures of the Bible*, published 1894.
    Copyright Â© 2003,2016 La Vista Church of Christ. Used by permission.
    http://www.lavistachurchofchrist.org/Pictures/Treasures%20of%20the%20Bible%20(Moses)/target26a.html

This book considers the Levitical offerings in the light of their fulfilment in the New Testament. It is designed as a self-study guide for individuals and groups who wish to improve their understanding of the Old Testament and its fulfilment in Christ.

ISBN 978-0-9925620-7-6

CONTENTS

1. THE BURNT OFFERING 5
ACCEPTANCE WITH GOD - LEVITICUS 1 5
1. THE OFFERING WAS PROVIDED BY THE PEOPLE 7
2. THE OFFERING WAS TO BE WITHOUT ANY DEFECT 8
3. GOD ACCEPTED THE OFFERING AS A SUBSTITUTE 10
4. THE OFFERING MAKES ATONEMENT FOR SIN 12
5. THE OFFERING IS PLEASING TO THE LORD 15
6. DIFFERENT WAYS OF THINKING ABOUT IT 16

2. THE GRAIN OFFERING 21
DEDICATION TO GOD - LEVITICUS 2:1-16 21
1. THE PREPARATION OF THE OFFERING 21
2. THE PRESENTATION OF THE OFFERING 29
3. PAUL'S CHALLENGE FOR ALL OF US TODAY 33

3. THE PEACE OFFERING 36
PEACE WITH GOD, SELF, THE WORLD - LEVITICUS 3:1-17 .. 36
1. PUT YOURSELF INTO THE PICTURE 36
2. FEATURES OF THE PEACE OFFERING 38
3. A COMMUNAL MEAL YET TO COME? 41
4. AN OFFERING MADE BY FIRE 42

4. THE SIN OFFERING 44
FORGIVENESS FOR ALL - LEVITICUS 4 – 5:13 44
1. EVEN FOR SINS THAT ARE NOT PLANNED 44
2. WHO IS THE SIN OFFERING PROVIDED FOR? 45
3. SALVATION FOR SOME OR FOR ALL PEOPLE? 51
4. SIN AND ITS EFFECTS 51

5. THE GUILT OFFERING 55
MAKING THINGS RIGHT - LEVITICUS 5:14-6:7 55
1. INTRODUCTION 55
2. WRONGS THAT SHOULD BE MADE RIGHT 55

1. THE BURNT OFFERING

ACCEPTANCE WITH GOD - Leviticus 1

Deep down inside us we have all felt a longing to be accepted. We want people around us who accept us, who help us grow in our physical, emotional and spiritual lives.

Dr Garry Collins[1] has this to say about the reason many people do not experience that acceptance:

> Parents communicate acceptance in a variety of ways; by touching, by spending time with their children, by listening, by discipline, by showing affection. When these clues are missing, or when children are ignored or excessively criticized, they begin to feel worthless. They begin to conclude that they don't belong and they either withdraw from others or force themselves on others in a way that brings more rejection. It then becomes difficult to trust people and this inability to trust prevents close relationships from forming.

We who are older respond in similar ways when we do not feel accepted. Parents who feel they are no longer accepted or wanted by their children, spouses who feel rejected by their mates, pastors who feel unappreciated by their congregations, or employees who feel shunned by their employers and co-workers—all are examples of people who feel unaccepted, not needed, and often lonely.

In your culture, what makes people feel that they are accepted or rejected?

✍

---

[1] Collins, Gary R. CHRISTIAN COUNSELLING. England: Word (UK) Ltd. 1988. pp. 95-96.

Rising Smoke – The Levitical Offerings

Are there times in which you personally do not feel accepted by the people around you? Why?

✎

An even deeper need we have is to feel that God accepts us. The people of Israel were able to find that acceptance through the sacrificial offerings.

📖 **Read Leviticus 1:1-17.**

What do you learn about finding acceptance with God from this chapter?

✎

Can we expect to find anything of significance today in the sacrifices described for us in Leviticus? Allen Ross[2] tells us that we can.

> The Biblical descriptions of sacrifices represent a complex system of ritual worship that is not entirely clear to the modern Reader. This is partly due to the texts legislating and describing activities that span centuries, naturally involving change and developing within the prescribed ritual. It is also due to the biblical accounts not explaining the meaning of much of the material, apparently assuming that people would either know by experience or learn through Levitical instruction the reasons for all the details (Deuteronomy 33:10, Malachi 2:7).
>
> For us, what has been made clear in Scripture provides a framework for the interpretation of the details … All the sacrifices that were given to Israel find their fulfilment in the death of the Son of God on the cross—that was the plan all along … And in

---

[2] Ross, Allen P. HOLINESS TO THE LORD. A Guide to the Exposition of the Book of Leviticus. Michigan: Baker Academic. 2002. pp. 29-30, 33.

the fullness of time their true significance became clear in God's plan of redemption.

As we come now to explore the features of the burnt offering, let's look for elements in it that point us to the sacrificial death of Christ.

📖 **Read carefully John's description of Jesus in John 1:29b.**

How does John describe Jesus? Compare this with Leviticus 1:10. Is there anything the same?

✎

Here are some features of the Burnt Offering to look for:

1. THE OFFERING WAS PROVIDED BY THE PEOPLE

📖 **Read Leviticus 1:2.**

The offering was to come from among the people—from the cattle, sheep, or birds they owned. What about Jesus, did he come from among the people?

✎

📖 **Read John 1:14 and Philippians 2:5-11.**

What do these verses tell us about Jesus and how he lived?

✎

2. THE OFFERING WAS TO BE WITHOUT ANY DEFECT

The people needed to choose the offering carefully. It was to be without a defect or blemish of any sort. We take this to mean in personality as well as physically. The Lord gives this further instruction to Moses to pass on to the people.

📖 **Read Leviticus 1:3 and 10.**

How does Jesus meet the requirements for the Leviticus offerings according to the following passages:

2 Corinthians 5:21

✍

1 Peter 1:18-20

✍

Hebrews 4:15

✍

Hebrews 9:13-14

✍

Rising Smoke – The Levitical Offerings

Notice how Peter in his letter tells us that God had planned 'long before the world began' that Christ would become the sacrificial offering for sin. John writes of him as 'the lamb who was killed before the world was made.' (Revelation 13:8b). This is why we can say that God saw the sacrificial death of Christ in the sacrificial offerings presented by the people of Israel. The sacrificial death of Christ was foreshadowed in those former offerings. One New Testament writer puts it this way …

> The old system in the law of Moses was only a shadow of the things to come, not the reality of the good things Christ has done for us. The sacrifices under the old system were repeated again and again, year after year, but they were never able to provide perfect cleansing for those who came to worship. (Hebrews 10:1)

📖 **Read Hebrews 10:11-12.**

The writer explains that Jesus did more than what the Old Testament priests did. They only presented an offering to God. He did more than that. Notice also how the writer refers to Christ as 'our High Priest.' As you think about the following question, can you see why?

As our High Priest, what has Jesus done for us?

✎

Forgiveness was still possible under the former system however, because God saw the sacrificial death of Christ on the cross pictured in those sacrifices.

3. GOD ACCEPTED THE OFFERING AS A SUBSTITUTE

📖 **Read Leviticus 1:4.**

The Concise Oxford Dictionary defines a substitute as 'a person performing some function instead of another,' or 'something put in exchange for something else.' In the burnt offering, the priest presented the sacrifice on behalf of the person. The animal took the death penalty instead of the person who had sinned.

What did people have to do in order for God to accept the sacrifice as a substitute for them?

✎

📖 **Read John 1:12.**

How does the Old Testament picture of Leviticus 1:4 help us understand what John says in this verse about Christ? How do we 'lay a hand' on him? Or to ask the question in another way, using John's language, 'What do we need to do to become a child of God?'

✎

Here's a question to think about while moving on in the study: Why is a substitute needed?

✎

Rising Smoke – The Levitical Offerings

📖 **Read Genesis 2:15-17, Ezekiel 18:4 and Romans 6:23.**

What does God say is the penalty for disobeying him?

✎

It is we sinful people who are under the sentence of death because of our sins. When Jesus Christ received the death penalty he took our place. He was there on the cross instead of us.

📖 **Read Isaiah 53:4-6, Romans 5:8-9 and 1 Corinthians 5:7.**

According to these verses, who did Jesus suffer and die for?

✎

📖 **Read again Leviticus 1:4**

Notice what the burnt offering accomplished for the people and how they responded. Laying hands on the burnt offering was the way people showed that they believed the sacrifice was being made on their behalf. It was an indication of faith. Faith brought the assurance that their sins were now atoned for. This is what the burnt offering is all about.

4. THE OFFERING MAKES ATONEMENT FOR SIN

How are we to understand the term 'atonement'? The Hebrew word is *kaphar*. Its basic meaning is 'to cover'. It is derived from the word *kopher*, 'the price of a life, a ransom.' Based on the meaning of these two Hebrew words, Charles Swindoll[3] defines atonement this way.

> ATONEMENT: An all-inclusive word that describes, in general, all that Jesus Christ accomplished by his death on the cross. The term is found only in the Old Testament, where it means 'to cover' and carries with it the thought of putting sin out of sight, covering it over by blood.

In the word atonement we find the idea of God's anger being satisfied by means of a sacrificial offering. The phrase, *'to satisfy God's anger against us'*, found here in the New Living Translation which follows, gives us the actual meaning of the word.

> For all have sinned and come short of God's glorious standard. Yet now God in his gracious kindness declares us not guilty. He has done this through Christ Jesus, who has freed [redeemed] us by taking away our sins. For God sent Jesus to take the punishment for our sins and to satisfy God's anger against us. (Romans 3:23-26).

We must remember that God is perfect in the expression of all his emotions whereas we are imperfect. In expressing his wrath or anger God remains holy. We are anything but perfect in the expression of ours. John Stott[4] helps us understand the nature of God's anger when he reminds us that 'sin arouses the wrath of God.'

> This does not mean, (as animists fear) that he is likely to fly off the handle at the most trivial provocation, still less that he loses his temper for no apparent reason at all. For there is nothing capricious or arbitrary about the holy God. Nor is he ever

---

[3] Swindoll, Charles R. GROWING DEEP IN THE CHRISTIAN LIFE. Oregon: Multnomah Press. 1986. p. 413.
[4] Stott, John. THE ESSENTIAL JOHN STOTT. Combined Edition. The Cross Of Christ. The Contemporary Christian. England: IVF. 1999. p. 160.

irascible, malicious, spiteful or vindictive. His anger is neither mysterious or irrational. It is never unpredictable, but always predictable, because it is provoked by evil and evil alone. The wrath of God ... is his steady, unrelenting, unremitting, uncompromising antagonism to evil in all its forms and manifestations. In short, God's anger is poles apart from ours. What provokes our anger (injured vanity) never provokes his; what provokes his anger (evil) seldom provokes ours.

The atonement made possible by the burnt offering has been fully realised in the sacrificial death of Christ.

📖 **Read 1 John 2:1-2.**

What does John say about Jesus' work of atonement?

✎

It is important to remember that it is God who takes the initiative in all of this. The atoning sacrifice, in both the burnt offering and Christ's sacrificial death, is a gift from God. It is God who is making the atoning sacrifice, not us. We do not present it, God does on our behalf. John Stott[5] explains it for us ...

> In a pagan context it is always human beings who seek to avert the divine anger either by the meticulous performance of rituals, or by the recitation of magical formulae, or by the offering of sacrifices (vegetable, animal, or even human). Such practices are thought to placate the offended deity. But the gospel begins with the outspoken assertion that nothing we can do, say, offer or even contribute can compensate for our sins or turn away God's anger. There is no possibility of persuading, cajoling or bribing God to forgive us, for we deserve nothing at his hands but judgement.

---

[5] ibid: Stott, John. p. 160.

Nor, as we have seen, has Christ by his sacrifice prevailed on God to pardon us. No, the initiative has been taken by God himself in his sheer mercy and grace.

This was already clear in the Old Testament, in which the sacrifices were recognized not as human works but as divine gifts. They did not make God gracious; they were provided by a gracious God in order that he might act graciously towards his sinful people. 'I have given it to you', God said of the sacrificial blood, 'to make atonement for yourselves on the altar' (Leviticus 17:11). And this truth is yet more plainly recognized in the New Testament, not least in the three main texts about propitiation (atonement).[6] God himself 'presented' (NIV) or 'put forward' (RSV) Jesus Christ as a propitiatory (atoning) sacrifice (Romans 3:25). It is not that we loved God, but that he loved us and sent his Son as a propitiation (atonement) for our sins (1 John 4:10). It cannot be emphasised too strongly that God's love is the source, not the consequence of the atonement.

As P. T Forsyth[7] expressed it, 'the atonement did not procure grace, it flowed from grace.' God does not love us because Christ died for us; Christ died for us because God loved us. If it is God's wrath that needed to be propitiated, it is God's love which did the propitiating.

In the comment above, John Stott is taking the word 'propitiation' from an old English translation of the Scriptures. The word carries the same meaning as the word 'atonement.'

---

[6] For Stott's use of the term 'propitiation', found in older translations, Read 'atoning sacrifice'.

[7] P. T. Forsyth, *Cruciality of the Cross,* p. 78. Compare Calvin's statement: 'The work of atonement derives from God's love, therefore it did not establish it' (*Institutes,* II.xvi.4).

5. THE OFFERING IS PLEASING TO THE LORD

God gave detailed instructions for the priests about how they were to present the burnt offering.

📖 **Read Leviticus 1:9-17.**

What are the priests instructed to do with the sacrifice?

✎

How does God feel about this sacrifice?

✎

📖 **Read Psalm 40:6-10 and Hebrews 10:1-10.**

What was it about the sacrifice that pleased God?

Was it the offering itself that God was pleased with, or something else? What can you find in the above Scriptures to answer this question?

✎

📖 **Read Hebrews 11:6.**

What do we need to do to please God?

✎

Rising Smoke – The Levitical Offerings

📖 **Read Psalm 51:10, 16-17.**

David realised the sinfulness of his recent life style and asked the Lord for forgiveness.

What does David tell us that God looks for in a person's attitude? How does he describe the kind of sacrifice that God is pleased with?

✎

You may be wondering just now what the people's response to the Lord's instructions concerning the burnt offering may have been. In such a large community we would expect that people would have ...

6. DIFFERENT WAYS OF THINKING ABOUT IT

6.1 A Superior Attitude

The offerings that poor people brought were just as acceptable to the Lord as those the wealthy brought. But some of the wealthier people who took their sacrificial offerings from the large herds they owned may have been tempted to look down on those who brought an offering from their small flock of sheep, or those who had only a bird to bring. They may have thought that they were superior because of the size of their herd or flock. An attitude like that could so easily lead to acts of discrimination in the community, like those which arose among some of the early Christians.

📖 **Read James 2:1-4.**

What does James say about discrimination? Is discrimination right? How do we discriminate against some people?

✎

People sometimes feel superior because of the status of the Christian leaders they follow or the denomination they belong to. Paul warned the members of the church in Corinth that this was just what was happening among them.

📖 **Read 1 Corinthians 3:3-5, 4:6-7.**

What does Paul say is the reason for these superior feelings? What does he say is the way to overcome those feelings?

✎

Others may feel superior because of the spiritual gifts they had received, forgetting that different gifts[8] are given to people according to the ministry they are called to fulfil. No particular gift makes one person superior to the other. Paul writes of this in another of his letters.

---

[8] Refer to Romans 12:6-8; 1 Corinthians 12:1-11, 27-31; Ephesians 4:4-13.

📖 **Read Romans 12:3-11.**

What advice does Paul give to those who feel superior because of the spiritual gifts they have received?

✍

6.2 Not Every Offering Is Acceptable to God

The animals offered were to be in perfect condition. But some people may have thought that it didn't matter what kind of offering they presented. For example, someone going out into the fields to choose an animal from the herd or flock might spot a sickly looking one and think, "that one is half dead anyway, it will do for the offering."

📖 **Read Psalm 50:7-15.**

What does God say in these verses about the sacrifices? Who owns the animals anyway? What does God really want?

✍

📖 **Read Malachi 1:6-10.**

What does God, through Malachi, say about the kind of sacrifices people were offering? How did God feel about this?

✍

6.3 Religious Syncretism

The term religious syncretism refers to the mixing of two or more religious beliefs and systems to try and gain maximum spiritual influence.

When they saw the way the Canaanites offered sacrifices to their gods, some of the Israelites may have thought it would be a good idea to mix what they considered to be the good elements of the Canaanite rituals with theirs.

It seems that religious syncretism created trouble for the church in Colosse. Both the Judaism of the Israelites and the Gnosticism of Greek philosophers had become entwined with Christian truth in the teaching of the false teachers who were troubling the members of the church. Herbert Carson[9] writes:

> The resultant religious amalgam (mixture) is an attempt to advance beyond apostolic Christianity. There is no suggestion that Christ is openly rejected. He still has a place; but only as one among many angelic powers.

Paul wrote to the church in Colosse to help them discern some of these errors.

📖 **Read Colossians 1:9-10, 2:6-10.**

Paul suggests several ways for the Christians in Colosse to remain strong in their faith. What are those ways?

---

[9] Carson, Herbert M. THE EPISTLES OF PAUL TO THE COLOSSIANS AND PHILEMON. Michigan: Tyndale Press. 1977. p. 17.

A PERSONAL REFLECTION

'Type' is a term given to refer to something that presents a picture of or represents something else. Allen Ross[10] tells us that "Typology is a divinely prefigured illustration of a corresponding reality." With this definition in mind think back over what you have discovered in this first chapter of Leviticus.

What new things have you learnt about the death of Christ? In the Burnt Offering, is there a 'type' of Christ, features that present us with a picture of him?

✍

What new perspectives on the meaning of faith for a Christian have you learnt?

✍

How can you apply what you have learnt about what pleases God to your life and attitudes?

✍

Do you now feel accepted by the Lord? Do you feel comfortable in God's presence now? What makes you feel this way?

✍

---

[10] ibid: Ross, Allen P. p. 96, footnote 23.

2. THE GRAIN OFFERING

DEDICATION TO GOD - Leviticus 2:1-16

The burnt offering opened the way to acceptance with God. The grain offering, also known as the meal offering, presents the way of declaring or renewing a person's dedication to God. Allen Ross[11] writes ...

> It is fitting for those God has accepted through sacrificial atonement to express their dedication to him. And this is the relationship between the meal offering and the burnt offering. The meal offering was an acknowledgement that everything the offerer had and was, belonged to God. And now a portion of that substance was to be given back to God as an expression of the belief that God was the source of and the provider of life.
>
> The main emphasis in an exposition of the meal offering should be its idea of dedication to God. The expectation is that those who have been reconciled to God and have access into his presence will regularly acknowledge that they owe everything to God—dedication follows atonement. This sacrifice gave the thankful Israelite worshipper the way to do it.

1. THE PREPARATION OF THE OFFERING

📖 **Read Leviticus 2:1.**

What are the ingredients that are used in preparing the offering?

---

[11] ibid: Ross, Allen P. p.p. 98-99.

Rising Smoke – The Levitical Offerings

Where did those ingredients come from? If you were the person preparing the offering, would you have had any part in producing them?

✍

The flour prepared from the grain is described as being choice, fine flour. The Hebrew word 'sōle_t_' describes flour that is free of husks. It is flour that is more costly to produce. It was more valuable than other kinds of flour. It was the kind of flour used in the household of a king, or when entertaining honoured guests.[12] This kind of flour therefore, is an appropriate choice for a person to use when preparing the grain offering to offer as an indication of their dedication to God. In choosing the more costly flour for the offering, is there a lesson there for anyone thinking about serving the Lord?

📖 **Read Luke 9:57-62, 14:25-33.**

In these selections, what is Jesus teaching those who are showing interest in following him?

✍

📖 **Read Philippians 3:1-11.**

Make a list of the things in his life that Paul gave up to follow the Lord.

✍

---

[12] Brown-Driver-Briggs Hebrew and English Lexicon. Unabridged Electronic data base.

Rising Smoke – The Levitical Offerings

📖 **Read Philippians 3:12-17.**

Do you think Paul ever regretted turning away from the things he valued then, to follow the Lord? What was it that replaced them? Was it more or less valuable?

✎

Notice how the people were to use oil and incense in the preparation of the grain offering (vs. 1b, 4). The Jewish Encyclopedia[13] traces the various ways in which the symbolism associated with their use has been understood in Jewish religious life and later in some branches of the Christian church. But let's turn to the Scriptures to see what some of the Biblical writers understood the symbolism to be for them.

📖 **Read Psalm 141:1-2, Revelation 8:1-4.**

What was significant about the use of incense for David and John?

✎

📖 **Read Psalm 23:5-6, 1 Samuel 16:11-13, Isaiah 61:1-3.**

What did David and Samuel experience from the use of oil? How did they feel?

✎

---

[13] Go to www.jewishencyclopedia.com (Search for oil, incense)

In the word picture he drew of the coming of Messiah how would you explain the way Isaiah used the symbolism associated with the use of oil?

✍

Leviticus 2:2-3 takes us forward to the presentation of the offering. We return to this later, but in the meantime there is more for us to learn from the preparation of the offering.

📖 **Read Leviticus 2:4-11.**

What was it that God did not want people to use in the grain offering?

✍

The yeast used in bread making then was in a different form from the yeast we use today. J. D. Douglas[14] tells us that the yeast "was probably a piece of dough, retained from a former baking which had fermented and turned acid. This was either dissolved in water in the kneading trough before the flour was added, or was hidden in the flour and kneaded along with it. Rabbinical writers often used yeast as a symbol of evil." The fermentation the yeast produces, causes the bread mixture to rise. The yeast works as an agent of change, out of sight, deep within the mixture.

---

[14] THE ILLUSTRATED BIBLE DICTIONARY. England: Inter-Varsity Press. 1980. (p. 891)

Honey too, writes Ross,[15] "may have been forbidden because it turns quickly to fermentation, causing corruption. If this is correct, then the prohibition about honey reinforced the main idea that a dedicatory offering must be without corruption."

Remembering that in the grain offering, people were indicating their dedication to God, can you think of any possible reasons for God not wanting yeast or honey to be part of the grain offering?

✍

 Read Matthew 16:5-12, Galatians 5:7-10, 1 Corinthians 5:1-8.

What was Jesus referring to when he warned his disciples about 'the yeast of the Pharisees?'

✍

Drawing his word picture from the way yeast works in a bread mixture, why was Paul concerned about what was happening in the churches in Galatia and Corinth?

✍

---

[15] ibid: Ross, Allen P. (p. 105)

Rising Smoke – The Levitical Offerings

All kinds of thoughts would be occupying the minds of those coming to the services in the tabernacle, just as there would be among people attending church services today. They come with anxious thoughts, sad or joyous thoughts, pure or sinful thoughts. Some come with minds fixed on the Lord, others with their thoughts elsewhere, those whose "thoughts either accuse them or tell them they are doing right."[16] Sadly, immoral thoughts can be fermenting in a person's mind, like the yeast in bread making, right there in the tabernacle, or in religious services today. Solomon provides us with an example of this very thing.

📖 **Read Proverbs 7:1-23.**

Where had this young lady been just before she met up with that young man? What had she been doing there? While doing that, what do you think may have been filling her thoughts? (vs. 14)

✎

📖 **Read Leviticus 2:4-7.**

Notice the several ways in which the people prepared their grain offerings. Do you think it mattered what method they used?

✎

---

[16] Refer to Romans 2:15.

📖 **Read 1 Corinthians 1:10-17.**

Paul was concerned about the way in which members of the house churches in Corinth were arguing among themselves. What do you think may have been contributing to the disagreement?

✍

Leviticus 2:8-10 continues the instructions for the presentation of the offering. But again we pass over those verses for now, while we learn some more about the preparations being made for its presentation.

📖 **Read Leviticus 2:11-13.**

What other ingredient for use in preparing the grain offering is mentioned in these verses?

✍

Allen Ross[17] writes of the significance of the use of salt in the grain offering:

> The emphasis most likely is on the nature of salt as a preservative. If that is the case, then the 'salt of the covenant' symbolised the preservation of the covenant between God and his people.[18]

---

[17] ibid: Ross, Allen P. (p. 105)
[18] Refer to Numbers 18:19, 2 Chronicles 13:5.

Rising Smoke – The Levitical Offerings

When covenants were made between tribal groups, each party ate the salt, which in some settings may even have been passed around on the edge of the blade of a sword. Those who 'tasted the salt' became covenant allies, or if 'salt was between them,' they were in covenant. The requirement of salt for the grain offering was filled with significance for the covenant people.

R. K. Harrison[19] adds: "It was often used among oriental peoples for ratifying agreements, so that salt became the symbol of fidelity and constancy."

The use of salt in the grain offering reminds us to preserve our dedication to the Lord, to keep it fresh and wholesome. But how do we maintain this freshness?

📖 **Read John 4:10-14, 7:37-39, Revelation 7:15-17, 21:5-7, 22:1-2, 17.**

In the word pictures John points us to, what do we see as the source of what we need to help us keep our dedication to the Lord alive and well? What do the pictures tell us about that source?

✎

📖 **Read 1 Corinthians 16:5-18.**

In our relationship with others, whether it be in the community or in the church, do you see anything Paul writes about here that relates to preserving your dedication to God.?

✎

---

[19] ibid: THE ILLUSTRATED BIBLE DICTIONARY. (p. 1370)

Rising Smoke – The Levitical Offerings

📖 **Read Ephesians 6:10-18, 2 Timothy 1:3-8.**

In these letters Paul draws his word pictures from the armour worn by a Roman soldier and a fire place. What do each of those items represent in the Christian life? How do they contribute to keeping our dedication to God fresh and meaningful?

✍

After completing all the preparatory work in getting their grain offerings ready to take to the tabernacle, the people are now ready for ...

2. THE PRESENTATION OF THE OFFERING

📖 **Read Leviticus 2:2-3, 8-10, 14-16.**

The people did not present their grain offerings directly to the Lord. Another person did that on their behalf. Who was that person?

✍

📖 **Read Hebrews 4:14-16.**

Later, God sent someone else to replace that person, the one who was 'appointed to represent them in matters related to God.'[20] Who is that someone else?

✍

---

[20] Hebrews 5:1. (NIV)

In presenting the grain offering, notice that the priest took the grain from two separate lots. There was firstly …

The Memorial Portion

📖 **Read Leviticus 2:2.**

The Hebrew noun translated as 'memorial offering,' is derived from the verb *zakar* 'to remember, be mindful of, take thought of.' Allen Ross[21] takes us a step further in understanding its meaning when he writes, "The idea of a memorial portion given to God goes beyond a simple reminding. The verb often carries the nuance[22] of beginning to act on the basis of what is remembered. The 'memorial portion' thus reminded worshippers to live according to the covenant obligations, that is, to live as if all they had, truly came from the Lord.'"

The 'memorial portion' of the grain offering points us forward to that last celebration of the Passover Meal Jesus had with his disciples.

📖 **Read Luke 22:7-20.**

As you Read through this account of the meal, was there anything in particular about it that stands out for you?

✍

When Jesus 'took a loaf of bread' and said, 'This is my body, given for you,' what does this mean for you?

✍

---

[21] ibid: Ross, Allen P. (p. 107)
[22] *nuance* 'A subtle shade of colour, expression, meaning, or feeling.' MACQUARIE. Australia's National Dictionary. Macquarie Publishers. 2009. (p. 859)

And later, when Jesus 'took another cup of wine,' and spoke of 'the blood I will pour out for you,' what do you think he meant by that phrase?

✍

How did the request Jesus made of his disciples change the significance of the Passover meal for them? What is the significance of that change for Christians today?

✍

Thinking about the way in which God has provided for the forgiveness of sins in Jesus' voluntary death on the cross as the sacrificial 'Lamb of God,'[23] does that make you want to confirm your dedication to the Lord?

✍

---

[23] Refer to John 1:29.

Rising Smoke – The Levitical Offerings

The second lot of grain the priest set aside from the grain offering was to provide ...

Support For The Priests

📖 **Read Leviticus 2:3, 10.**

What do you think? Does this seem a fair way to provide food for the priests?

✎

This second lot of the grain offering set aside to provide food for the priests brings us to the question of how those in Christian ministry today should be supported.

📖 **Read** Acts 18:1-3, Philippians 4:10-20, 1 Corinthians 9:1-19.

What was Paul's attitude to receiving financial support?

✎

Do Paul's references to the way in which he received his income inform your thinking about how Christian workers ought to be supported today?

✎

As we conclude this study, let's take time before we move on to think about ...

3. PAUL'S CHALLENGE FOR ALL OF US TODAY

📖 **Read Romans 12:1-2.**

What do think Paul is saying when he invites his Readers 'to present your bodies a living and holy sacrifice acceptable to God?' What does he have in mind as he draws this word picture? (vs. 1)

✍

What changes start to appear in the lives of those who respond to Paul's challenge? (vs. 2)

✍

It is always helpful to notice how others respond to such a challenge.

📖 **Read Genesis 12:1-8, Hebrews 11:8, Exodus 3:4, Hebrews 11:24-28, 1 Samuel 3:10, Hebrews 11:32-35, Acts 26:12-19, 28.**

How did Abraham, Moses, Samuel, Paul, and Agrippa reply to God's call upon their lives? Are there words or phrases in any of their responses that you would use in your answer as Paul dares us to confirm the dedication of our lives to serve the Lord?

✍

Abraham:

Rising Smoke – The Levitical Offerings

Moses:

Samuel:

Paul:

Agrippa:

A PERSONAL REFLECTION

Francis Havergal[24] expressed her decision in the writing of this song.

> Take my life and let it be
> Consecrated, Lord, to Thee.
> Take my moments and my days,
> Let them flow in endless praise.
>
> Take my hands and let them move
> At the impulse of Thy love.
> Take my feet and let them be
> Swift and beautiful for Thee.
>
> Take my voice and let me sing,
> Always, only for my King.
> Take my lips and let them be
> Filled with messages from Thee.
>
> Take my silver and my gold,
> Not a mite would I withhold.
> Take my intellect and use
> Every power as Thou shalt choose
>
> Take my will and make it Thine,
> It shall be no longer mine.
> Take my heart, it is Thine own,
> It shall be Thy royal throne.
>
> Take my love, my Lord, I pour
> At Thy feet its treasure store.
> Take myself and I will be
> Ever, only, all for Thee.

What about you?

✍

---

[24] http://library.timelesstruths.org/music/

3. THE PEACE OFFERING

PEACE WITH GOD, SELF, THE WORLD - Leviticus 3:1-17

One significance of the peace offering is that it celebrated the sense of well being enjoyed by the worshippers as a result of the forgiveness their sins, the acceptance of the Lord and the dedication of their lives to him. As F. Duane Lindsey[25] explains,

> The presentation of the offering was conditioned on a worshipper's having first met the requirements of expiation (through a sin or guilt offering) and dedication (through burnt and grain offerings).

As we look into the chapter …

1. PUT YOURSELF INTO THE PICTURE

📖 **Read Leviticus 3.**

Imagine yourself to be among those participating in the tabernacle service that day.

What would you be doing?

✍

Describe the part being played by the priests?

✍

---

[25] The Bible Knowledge Commentary (OT). (p. 178)

Do you notice anything in the sacrifices being presented that is similar to a religious service you may be part of?

✍

After taking part in the celebration of the peace offering that day, how do you think people may have felt as they left the tabernacle?

✍

📖 **Read Acts 8:26-38.**

How did the treasurer in the government of Ethiopia feel as he left for home after attending the service in Jerusalem? What was it that was troubling him?

✍

How did Philip help the treasurer?

✍

How do you feel as you head home after the church services or meetings you attend each week?

✍

2. FEATURES OF THE PEACE OFFERING

Notice firstly that part of the peace offering was set aside for the people to enjoy as a ...

A COMMUNAL MEAL

This feature of the peace offering emerges when we come to the further instructions given to the priests regarding the offerings.

📖 **Read Leviticus 7:11-15.**

Allen Ross[26] draws our attention to the significance of this further instruction regarding the Peace Offering.

> Leviticus 7 will emphasise that the worshipper and the congregation ate part of the sacrifice. So this sacrifice, the celebration of being at peace with God, was considered a communal meal eaten in the presence of the Lord.
>
> All of this ritual was one of the greatest expressions of communion with God. That the communal meal was received from the sacrifice is striking. In almost all the other sacrifices it was the offerer giving to God, but here it is as if God was returning portion of the offering for the faithful to eat in his presence. This indicates the Lord's gracious bounty to his people and the peaceful relationship that existed within the covenant.

Scrolling through the Scriptures, we also notice that the peace/fellowship offering was often ...

PRESENTED AT A TIME OF CELEBRATION

📖 **Read 1 Kings 8:54-66.**

What was it that made this such a happy occasion for the people of Israel?

✎

---

[26] ibid: Ross, Allen P. (pp. 118-119)

Can you recall an event in your community or church that would call for such a celebration?

✎

The celebration of the peace offering with its communal meal to follow, also became ...

A TIME OF FELLOWSHIP

Considered as a communal meal, we see in the peace offering another feature of the communion service pictured previously for us in the grain offering. There the 'token portion' drew our attention to the memorial aspect of the communion service. But now we see that a prominent feature in the picture is that of fellowship. With this in mind, the communion service, or as it is sometimes called, the Eucharist, becomes for us not only a memorial of Christ's sacrificial death on our behalf, but a special time of fellowship with him and with each other. My wife and I always enjoyed our visits to a country church in South Australia. A typical country style lunch following the service morphed just so naturally into the communion service. It was a rich experience of fellowship with each other and the Lord. Allen Ross[27] offers this comment ...

> For Christians the great joy of being at peace with God through Jesus Christ is captured by the celebration of the communal meal of the new covenant, the Lord's Supper, which is rightly called Eucharist–thanksgiving ... Both the animal of the peace offering and the elements of the communion service represent the true sacrifice, the person, Jesus the Messiah ... Those who have been redeemed and have given their lives to the Lord will spontaneously participate in communal acts of worship ... To

---

[27] ibid: Ross, Allen P. (pp. 120-121)

them, the Lord's Table will be a wonderful experience of celebration by which they attest that they are at peace with God.

 📖 **Read Acts 2:41-47.**

What do you think those first Christian believers may have been thinking about as they shared in the Lord's supper at that time?

✎

What are the three characteristics of life in the early church that are highlighted here?

✎

How important do you think that Christian fellowship would have been for those first century Christians?

✎

 📖 **Read 1 John 1:5-7.**

How much of a challenge do John's words present to members of your church?

✎

3. A COMMUNAL MEAL YET TO COME?

The communal meal of the peace offering points us to the final Passover meal the Lord had with his disciples. As the meal progressed, Jesus presented himself as the sacrificial Lamb of God.[28] Within the familiar scene of the Passover meal, did he also suggest that he would be preparing yet another communal meal for us at some later time?

📖 **Read Luke 22:7-20.**

What do you think Jesus may have had in mind, when he said of the communal meal he was sharing with his disciples, "I tell you now that I won't eat it again until it comes to fulfilment in the Kingdom of God" (vs. 16).

✎

📖 **Read Revelation 19:4-10.**

What do see in the word picture John draws for us here? Is the 'wedding feast of the Lamb' that ultimate communal meal Jesus looked forward to?

✎

---

[28] As described in John 1:29.

One last feature of the peace offering catches our attention as we look over the chapter once more. It was to be …

4. AN OFFERING MADE BY FIRE

📖 **Read Leviticus 3.**

The phrase 'an offering made by fire,' (sometimes referred as 'an offering given to the Lord by fire,') occurs several times in the offerings we have been exploring. But it was in this account of the peace offering that I noticed it particularly. The phrase got me thinking when I remembered something Jesus said to his disciples.

📖 **Read Mark 9:49-50.**

When Jesus said that 'Everyone will be salted with fire,' what are your first thoughts about what he could have meant?

✎

Now turn to a letter Peter wrote for circulation among Christians who had moved to different provinces because of the waves of persecution that had begun to roll over and around them.

📖 **Read 1 Peter 1:4-7, 4:12-19.**

When Peter writes about 'being tested as fire tests and purifies gold,' and talks about 'fiery trials,' does this contribute to your understanding of what Jesus' words 'salted by fire,' may mean for you?

✎

A PERSONAL REFLECTION

And now as you go on your way, here is a great promise from the Lord to take with you. Given first to the people of Israel, it is now extended to include everyone who puts their trust in him. Being 'salted with fire'? Take courage and keep on going in your walk with the Lord!

> *The LORD who created you says, "Do not be afraid, for I have ransomed you. I have called you by name. You are mine. When you go through deep waters and great trouble, I will be with you. When you go through rivers of difficulty, you will not drown! When you go through the fire of oppression, you will not be burned up, the flames will not consume you. For I am the LORD your God."*
>
> *(Isaiah 43:1-3a)*

How does this promise help you to keep going in times of difficulty?

✎

4. THE SIN OFFERING

FORGIVENESS FOR ALL - Leviticus 4 – 5:13

1. EVEN FOR SINS THAT ARE NOT PLANNED

📖 **Read Leviticus 4:1-2.**

While the sin offering sits comfortably alongside the former offerings to provide for the forgiveness of all kinds of sins, the instructions for the sin offering begin by drawing our attention specifically to its provision for the forgiveness of sins committed without thought.

Allen Ross[29] references Wenham[30] as he introduces the chapter to us. He states:

> God, by his grace, made provision for cleansing sin and its effects so that people might safely enter his presence. This provision was absolutely necessary given the circumstances of life in this world. Sinful acts and defiled conditions of any kind must be dealt with if communion with God is to be maintained.
>
> Even true worshippers, people who are steadfast in their devotion to the Lord and who seek to live in obedience to his laws, find that they need God's gracious provision of cleansing if they are to continue in fellowship with him.
>
> They may fall into sin without realising it, or they may be overtaken with a fault, or they may sin unwittingly. But even these sins should not be treated lightly.

---

[29] ibid: Ross, Allen P. (123)
[30] Wenham, G. J. The Book of Leviticus. New International Commentary on the Old Testament. Grand Rapids: Eerdmans, 1979. (p. 89)

2. WHO IS THE SIN OFFERING PROVIDED FOR?

📖 **Read Leviticus 4:3-35.**

Several groups of people are mentioned in these opening instructions for the sin offering. Who are they? Is anyone left out?

✎

FALLING SHORT OF GOD'S STANDARD

Paul reminds us that we all fall short of the standard God has set for his people when he writes …

> We are all made right in God's sight when we trust in Jesus Christ to take away our sins. And we can all be saved in this same way, no matter who we are or what we have done. For all have sinned. All fall short of God's glorious standard. (Romans 3:22-23)

📖 **Read Leviticus 5:1-4.**

This portion of Scripture draws our attention to at least three ways in which a person's conduct may fall short of what it ought to be. Notice firstly …

The Failure To Testify (vs. 1)

The Macquarie Dictionary tells us that to testify is "to bear witness, to give or afford evidence, to make a solemn declaration, to give testimony under oath or solemn affirmation, usually in court, to bear witness to; affirm as fact or truth, to declare, profess, or acknowledge openly."[31]

What is expected of anyone who is asked to testify about something?

✎

---

[31] MACQUARIE, ibid: (p.1306)

Rising Smoke – The Levitical Offerings

For the people of Israel at that time, what do you think may have been some of the situations that would call for witnesses? If a person refused to testify when asked to do so, why do think God would consider that to be such a serious matter?

✍

For us today, as members of the community in which we live, in what circumstances could we ever be called on to give testimony?

✍

In the six days before his death, Jesus devoted much of his time to teaching his disciples. And now as the cross began to loom large in the hours just ahead of him, he turned to explaining the nature of the new relationship they would enjoy with him after his death and resurrection.

📖 **Read John 15:26-27.**

In this new relationship what role does the Holy Spirit play? And what does Jesus ask his followers to do?

✍

We often fail to take advantage of the many opportunities that come our way to do what Jesus has asked us to do. But just as

God provided forgiveness in the sin offering for a refusal to testify, so there is forgiveness for us too when we fail to bear witness to Christ, or as Eugene Peterson translates the phrase, when we fail to 'give ... confirming evidence' about him. Where do we find this forgiveness today after we fail to testify as we should?

📖 **Read 1 John 2:1-2.**

Who is Paul referring to when he says 'there is someone to plead for you before the Father?'

✍

Why is this person qualified to 'plead for you before the Father?'

✍

We come now to another of the ways in which our conduct may fall short of what it ought to be.

Touching The Unclean (vs. 2-3)

For the people of Israel, something unclean referred firstly to something associated with the sacrifices, such as an animal that had defects and was therefore unacceptable for the offering (vs. 2). Use of the unclean thing in an offering made for 'ceremonial uncleanness.' The unclean thing could also refer to something associated with bodily functions (vs. 3).

Touching the unclean thing produced overwhelming feelings of guilt for the person concerned, a sense of defilement. Presentation of the sin offering opened the way for forgiveness, a way to feel clean, to feel whole again.

What about us today? Are there things that the mere touching of them produces feelings of guilt within us? Paul has much to say about this. For an example …

📖 **Read 2 Corinthians 6:14-18.**

In this part of his letter Paul is drawing a series of contrasts between various items, such as between light and darkness (vs. 14b). What are some of the others he describes?

✎

What do you think could be some of the things that Paul may have been thinking of when he exhorts his readers, "Don't touch their filthy things?" (vs. 17)

✎

The sin offering also provides the way of forgiveness for …

The Broken Promise (vs. 4)

This verse is speaking to us about the promises we make to God. Like, for example, those the people of Israel made in response to Joshua's challenge as they began to take possession of the land God had set aside for them …

> "So honour the LORD and serve him wholeheartedly. Put away forever the idols your ancestors worshipped when they lived beyond the Euphrates River and in Egypt. Serve the LORD alone.
>
> But if you are unwilling to serve the LORD, then choose today who you will serve. Would you prefer the gods your ancestors served beyond the Euphrates? Or will it be the gods of the

Amorites in whose land you now live? But as for me and my family, we will serve the LORD."

The people replied, "We would never forsake the LORD and worship other gods. (Joshua 24:14-16)

How quickly the people forgot their promise, for in the historical account that follows, we read of the time when …

Again the Israelites did evil in the LORD's sight. They worshipped images of Baal and Ashtoreth, and the gods of Aram, Sidon, Moab, Ammon, and Philistia. Not only this, but they abandoned the LORD and no longer served him at all. (Judges 10:6)

The laws God gave to Moses for the wellbeing of his people make clear to all of us the sinfulness of failing to keep our promises. But at the same time they remind us to think carefully before promising something.

When you make a vow to the LORD your God, be prompt in doing whatever you promised him. For the LORD your God demands that you promptly fulfil all your vows. If you don't, you will be guilty of sin.

However, it is not a sin to refrain from making a vow. But once you have voluntarily made a vow, be careful to do as you have said, for you have made a vow to the LORD your God. (Deuteronomy 23:21-23)

📖 **Read Ecclesiastes 5:4-7.**

What is Solomon's advice regarding the making of promises?

✎

Solomon's reminder to his people may well have come from the memory of his step brother Absalom's deceitful use of a vow. Check it out as you …

Rising Smoke – The Levitical Offerings

📖 **Read 2 Samuel 15:1-12.**

What was Absalom's real reason in asking for David's approval to go to Hebron? What did he do when he got there?

✎

While not lowering the standards set by the Mosaic laws, Jesus takes us to another level. When teaching in Galilee on one occasion, he took his disciples aside from the crowds to what he hoped would be a quiet spot in the mountains. He taught them personally how he wanted them to carry out the intent of the Mosaic laws in their conduct as his disciples. What a wonderful mountain retreat with Jesus that must have been for his disciples. Among the topics he covered that day we find his comments about the making of a vow.

📖 **Read Matthew 5:33-37 and James 5:12.**

As Jesus taught his disciples there in the mountains that day, what do you think he is wanting them to learn about making promises? As the disciple James listened carefully, did he catch the meaning do you think?

✎

3. SALVATION FOR SOME OR FOR ALL PEOPLE?

📖 **Read Leviticus 5:5-13.**

What do think? Does forgiveness come in different portions for different classes of people depending on what they are able to offer?

✎

📖 **Read Luke 24:47.**

What did Jesus say? Is salvation just for a few select people? If not, then who is it for?

✎

Before moving on to the guilt offering, let's take a few more minutes to think about …

4. SIN AND ITS EFFECTS

When conduct in any way falls short of what it ought to be, it not only affects the person who has sinned, but it can also have an affect in at least three other ways.

The Effect of Sin in the Community

📖 **Read Joshua 7:19-21, 25a.**

What was the sin that brought shame on the people of Achan's community?

✎

Do you think the penalty handed out to Achan was too harsh? What do you think should be the consequences for breaking the law?

✍

Is there any kind of conduct that is bringing shame on your community? If there is something, what do you think can be done about it?

✍

The Effect of Sin on a Person's Position in the Community
📖 **Read Nehemiah 13:23-29.**

What was it that upset Nehemiah so much? Why do you think it mattered?

✍

What about people who hold positions of trust in your community? Is there anything bothering you about their conduct?

✍

Defilement of the Places People Visit

The Lord speaks, for example, of places of worship becoming defiled by the sin of any of its people. When God's people sin, God is grieved because of the effect their sins have on the atmosphere in the house of worship.

📖 **Read Ezekiel 5:5-11.**

What was it in Jerusalem at this time that was causing the Lord so much grief? In particular, where was it all happening?

✍

What about the places of worship in your part of the world? Do you see any need for change anywhere there? If so what would you like it to be?

✍

A PERSONAL REFLECTION

How do you feel about the way you may or may not be contributing to the well being of those you live, work and socialise with each day? Do you need to change anything?

5. THE GUILT OFFERING

MAKING THINGS RIGHT - Leviticus 5:14-6:7

1. INTRODUCTION

All of the offerings so far have had to do with repentance and God's forgiveness of sin, made possible because of the sacrifices presented. The guilt offering however takes us a step further. As well as asking the Lord for forgiveness, presenting the guilt offering indicated to him that the person's repentance was real and that they had made things right with any person they had done wrong to, that they had made reparation. Reparation may be understood as being "the act of repairing something broken, of making amends, the giving of compensation for a wrong committed."[32] Allen Ross,[33] who for those reasons, prefers to call this the reparation offering, writes ...

> The main point is that reparation is evidence of true repentance. Although God makes provision by his grace for forgiveness and restoration of the guilty, he requires genuine repentance as a prerequisite for forgiveness. Showing remorse for sin is not sufficient in the case where the wrong can be corrected. Making reparation is required in those situations.

2. WRONGS THAT SHOULD BE MADE RIGHT

The wrongs described in the guilt offering point us in two directions, to those committed against the Lord and to those against people. It each case the wrong involves defrauding in some way. To defraud someone is to deprive them of some right or

---

[32] Refer to MACQUARIE. ibid: (p. 1066)
[33] ibid: Ross, Allen P. (p. 147)

property by fraud, to take something from them by deceiving them in some way, by trickery.³⁴ Firstly ...

WRONGS AGAINST THE LORD

📖 **Read Leviticus 5:14-19.**

What is it that the people were defrauding the Lord of?

✎

What did God invite them to do about it?

✎

You may be wondering by now, just what is meant by the phrase 'the Lord's holy things,' or 'property' as the New Living Translation puts it? We find help and application for ourselves as we turn to some of the Scriptures that touch on our question.

📖 **Read Malachi 3:6-10.**

In its introduction to Malachi, the Ryrie Study Bible³⁵ refers us to the quality of the spiritual life of the people existing at the time the book was written.

> About 100 years had passed since the return of the Jews to Palestine. The city of Jerusalem and the second Temple had been built, but initial enthusiasm had worn off. Following a period of revival under Nehemiah,³⁶ the people and priests had backslidden and become mechanical in their observance of the Law ... they could not understand why God was dissatisfied with them.

---

³⁴ Refer to MACQUARIE. ibid: (p. 326)
³⁵ THE RYRIE STUDY BIBLE. Chicago: Moody Press, 1978. (p. 1430)
³⁶ Refer to Nehemiah 10:28-39.

Does the spiritual life of the people at that time resemble in any way that of the times in which we live?

✍

In the verses we are looking at, what is said about one of the ways in which the people were defrauding (cheating on, robbing) God?

✍

John Calvin points us to another of the possible ways in which we may defraud God when he writes ...

> "For we unjustly defraud God of his right unless each of us lives and dies in dependence on his sovereign pleasure."[37]

A glimpse into the life of Habakkuk may be helpful in teasing out an understanding of Calvin's comment.

📖 **Read Habakkuk 1:1-11.**

Habakkuk was a prophet in Israel at a time of Babylonian expansion across the Middle East and political unrest in Israel.[38]

How would you describe Habakkuk's feelings as he writes in his diary that day? What do you think was his attitude towards God as he prays?

✍

---

[37] Calvin, John TRACTS & LETTERS. Vol. 6. Banner of Truth Publisher February 2009. (p. 236)
[38] For the time of Habakkuk's writing refer to 2 Kings 23:34-24:5 and Jeremiah 22:13-19.

What do you learn about God from his reply to Habakkuk, especially in vs. 5-6a?

✍

With those verses in mind ...

📖 **Read Daniel 2:19-21 and Acts 17:22-27.**

What are Daniel and Paul saying about the Lord, Daniel in his prayer, and Paul in his address to the Council of Philosophers in Athens?

✍

Do you think Daniel and Paul could have been thinking about any of God's attributes in particular?

✍

Thinking again about Calvin's comment, in the light of the scriptures that we have been looking at, can you think of just one word to complete this sentence?

✍

God is _____

📖 **Read Matthew 6:25-34.**

There on that mountain side that day, what is Jesus teaching us?

✎

If we are constantly worrying about things that are happening in our world, globally and personally, what do you think we could be defrauding God of? Can you complete the following sentence with just one word?

We could be defrauding God of his

✎

_____

While exploring further in the Scriptures it may be that other ways of defrauding God will begin to emerge.

📖 **Read Psalm 139:13-16.**

In this stanza of his song, notice how David is praising the Lord as the one who has "made all the delicate, inner parts of my body and knit me together in my mother's womb. Thank you for making me so wonderfully complex. Your workmanship is marvellous—and how well I know it." (vs. 13-14)

If David had been referring to some 'other' as making him 'so wonderfully complex' would he have been defrauding God of his creativity? What do you think?

✎

Following on with this line of reasoning, as other attributes of God come to mind, do you see any other ways in which defrauding God may occur?

The guilt offering is also called for in the case of ...

WRONGS AGAINST PEOPLE

📖 **Read Leviticus 6:1-7.**

This section begins by telling us that the wrongs done to other people are also sins against the Lord. Why should this be so do you think?

✍

As it was with defrauding the Lord, the five wrongs against people that are spoken of here have to do with taking something from them. What are those five wrongs? (vs. 1-3)

✍

What should those who have defrauded someone of something do about it? (vs. 4-7)

✍

Have you noticed any of the ways in which people may be defrauding others in your community?

Notice that in the instructions God gave to Moses, the actual presentation of the guilt offering comes after reparation has been made. Do you think there is any significance in the order here, that offering compensation is put before presenting the guilt offering? While thinking about the question ...

📖 **Read Luke 3:1-20.**

Does the order John insist on for those wanting to take part in the baptismal ceremony inform your thinking in any way?

📖 **Read Matthew 5:23-24.**

Before offering a sacrifice to God, what does Jesus say should be done? Does this help in your thinking about the significance of the order evident in the instructions given for the guilt offering? What does this significance mean for you?

A Personal Reflection

The instructions for the guilt offering end with this assurance for the people '...and they will be forgiven.' What does God's forgiveness mean for you?

✎

This completes our survey of God's instructions for the five sacrificial offerings: the burnt, grain, peace, sin, and guilt offerings.

In our next book we take a look at the instructions God gave to the priests regarding the presentation of the offerings and to how they should be living as ordained priests of the Lord.

Email the author at nengebooks1@gmail with your feedback on this study.

See http://nengebooks.com for other books published by NENGE BOOKS.

www.ingramcontent.com/pod-product-compliance
Lightning Source LLC
Chambersburg PA
CBHW052136010526
44113CB00036B/2277